correction line

correction line

dennis cooley

for george baldwin, hidden poet,
in his own search for ancestors

in best friendship
dennis cooley
oct/88

thistledown press

Thistledown Press Ltd.
633 Main Street, Saskatoon, SK   S7H 0J8
www.thistledownpress.com

Library and Archives Canada Cataloguing in Publication
Cooley, Dennis, 1944–
Correction line / Dennis Cooley.
Poems.
ISBN 978-1-897235-50-8
I. Title.
PS8555.O575C67 2008   C811'.54   C2008-904522-X

Publisher Cataloging-in-Publication Data (U.S)
Cooley, Dennis.
Correction line / Dennis Cooley.
[96] p. : cm.
Summary: A poem sequence that reconstructs memory through pinpoint ancestral connections and personal history.
ISBN: 978-1-897235-50-8 (pbk.)
1. Canadian poetry -- 21st century. I. Title.
811.6 dc22 PR3603.O6Co 2008

Cover photograph © Klaus Leidorf/zefa/Corbis
Cover and book design by Jackie Forrie
Printed and bound in Canada

10 9 8 7 6 5 4 3 2 1

Thistledown Press gratefully acknowledges the financial assistance of the Canada Council for the Arts, the Saskatchewan Arts Board, and the Government of Canada through the Book Publishing Industry Development Program for its publishing program.

With thanks to Susan Musgrave, whose meticulous reading and whose sage advice has saved me from more than one embarrassment. At times not heeding her wise words, I have persisted in the errors of my ways.

Some of these pieces have appeared, in different versions, in *NeWest Review*, *Sunfall*, *passwords*, *perishable light*, and in *Our Fathers: Poetry and Prose by daughters and sons from the prairies*.

CONTENTS

my father's place

I think of his language

I learn how to speak it again
to say it again
to say it as he must have
the new remarkable works

                              and in Saskatchewan

                              correction line

imagine the end of
the beginning of
the lines

—Eli Mandel, *Life Sentence*

in memory of Eli Mandel
(1922-1992)
first Estevan poet

on the way to estevan
(thanksgiving saturday)

thistle in ditches
wait with dirt of the thirties
    silent
as children   when they listen
    in winds
    on water   from run off
    sun & sounds
                trapped
    as march is
  in nails of winter

railroad embankments rank with weeds
edges of fields corners off barnyards
perimeters that cling like kids to hockey
rinks small cracks in parking lots
patches in storage yards
trucks & cement & pipes & broken
  cars hold together
where weed seeds augur
  furrows of brains
  we embrace give
    birth to vulgar
    bursts of purple

this is our country
    it is here we fall
        into place
in it we
        let loose
  rain down in wind

all rights of way
    clicking with razors
dreams whistling with thistle

remembering

It should work.
all the leaves their first
coming little boats in may
before they perk like nipples
wanting to feel the rain & the air.

It should matter.
a man dozing in an undershirt
thinks of wind dreams of minnows
the windows he steps behind
waiting for breath.

It should
make a difference.
you think it's someone else
a disjointed bird standing there
winching itself to dignity
on the suspicions of all five toes
the slough loose around its ankles
the disappointed face

You think
they must be.
I have wanted to swim
summoned out of sight
up the souris
past the bridge you had
to reach in the red
cross tests return from
& one man fell
with his gravel
truck through to
drown.

It could be.
an adage old age
the edge of the water
the toe marks
birds who cry
when the shock
presses them
into the stench when
gravity takes them

It has to be.
the still water
under which they see
your face looking
the man who fell
through the sun felt the sun
fizzing in his mind went through
clouds that crowded his cranium
along broken pathways blood took

It might be.
geraniums, familiar & thick
when I take time to my head
a long wick burning
gather it there
& blow

all the candles out
all the ticking away

when the sky closed
and the wind broke loose your father
collapsed like a broken collar

grampa wilson fishing

i.

the 3 jack 2 small 1 larger my grampa
wilson pulls 38 years out of the souris
slow bend at Possum's even then must
have been sour with heat and sludge though I
                    remember it as sweet

their slow suspension on the chain
the brain in which memory moves
            a small boat
the day forms in water
the float & darkgreen
mucous of their buoyance

sun holds it all—frogs fish
river a grampa and a boy—
                tugged into place
begins to spool out in strings
astringent against night

                            a yank &
                on the bank they
                gasp where we have
                        pulled them
                out of the water we cannot
                        see far into
                heft of them in our hands
                their slippery moving
                the long smooth muscle
                the music of their lives
                or so it seems now to me

                the dust they flop & coat in
                sun so hot it could cook them

3 jacks in the trunk leak
                their lives
among tires & wrenches
their valves yanked out
the fish gulp & fill up on air

ii.

            smell of heavy dust the garage
                whose sudden darkness
        we roll the big black
                    car into
                            smell of gasoline
            all the garbage of heat
                    & corks hanging in the peppered light

        & later/ preparing supper
                when we are scaling
                        one of the little jacks
            starts swimming
            the slow & muddy water
                    in my mind

iii.

& my gramma in the other room the smell of lilies
        slaps you in the face
    sheets stuffed with perfume
who will die inside her broken hip
her small voice crying *henry henry*

consider how the brain resembles

the slough or maybe more the pot
       hole at the end
our lane where the ditch backed up
every spring because
there was no culvert

& the water sat there
   a fat lady
on the porch paralyzed
by heat & rats

but what there really was
was this
        grey scum
  all over the water & on it   walked
     myriads of eyes & wings
they : squirts of ink: shimmied
   & scrawled on some
madness of fever   all over that dirty skin
      quicksilver bent   under their passing

         & then the mosquitoes
chimed up like gothic
    script you might say
tensed on parchment   chimera
when the camera stills them

      & I have thot a lot
       about that since
     it seems to be a big
      metaphor for something   deep
     but it wasn't   really
     anything more   than that

you want me to say   huge
pike wallowed savagely   suddenly
out of murk shoved their
ugly snouts into the light
& busted the thin skin like a balloon
or a failed safe you want
something deep & dark
& you are wondering
         where is it
    when will it   appear
but there wasnt   there almost never is
a nasty jack clicking below

         you want significance
         you are wondering

how did this poem   get published

         but there was   only me   & my sisters
        & the 95° Estevansun
       lowering ourselves
          great
        —skysmooth as a babys bum—
            fully (we were
      parched(into
         —to the chin—
    of cold)   muddyhole
        at the end of our lane

family album

scraps of light locked
the looks they hope & wear
from their necks
look out steadily at no one

a question of could they
go over there the other
side of sun

time waxes their faces
yellow as old floors
heavy as air
in the closed rooms
less certain than furniture
more porous id guess
than curtains
their dust

trees at the window
are drinking
the slow light
must even then
have peeled the skin
what they were
must have touched
night's face, not knowing

the light,   their faces

iris

the light in the wood is the wood
itself you cannot tell
is it the birch wood the oil or sun
smooth slide of light / shadow
shad
             ow
\ sun
the striking laminations
you always loved
in your room the window
morning & night
moving across

ingathering where time congregates
in sun & shadow
while you in Chicago bend
blow dust off the lens of your camera

the lines we upstairs disassemble
& downstairs light
resembles nothing we can name
where it passed from a bright eye
through rows of eyeglasses
through which light & shadows fall
in the pictures you took and love

iris you call her
the figure through your mind
light & dark its liquid slide
quick and mobile vireo
in the video you constantly
assemble & reassemble
held an eye up to your eye
you have kept
a close eye on her

i sir i say i am iris o sir i am
iris i may be isis

light across the wet film of your eye dissembling
and thousands more   eyeglasses in auschwitz
the frightening beauty of their assembling
the window full of prosthetics vacated by bodies
heavy and cumbersome the lost legs & arms & crutches
        people must have moved like crushed creatures in & out of

                    emblems of fitting
                    downstairs move
                    the desk you sat at
                    aperture of your eye
                    opened & closed at

                blow all the dust you had dropt
                    lean over the desk
            your mother & i reassembling like weeds

rub the room with the smell of lemon
        oil over the desk &
                            /light
            jumps from the oak
lifting & gathering

                                    have to screw it down
                                keep all that light
                            from escaping

ploughing

1

how did you   get the lines
so straight my   uncle asked
        amazed   I hadn't
    lapsed or   drifted badly
it must have been   may
        I was   ploughing
    his past   it was
    64 i think   i would have been
    20 later   that year on his 44
    Massey & it   caught
fire when it was   ping
    ing & snor   ting i was in the mid
    dle before   i was done
    before i had   writ
    ten the last   furrow
    working from   row to row
behind me the past   ure was turning black

        a carbon copy   of winter
        a long banner   unfurling lines
            that said   summer
        that summer   summer fall
                o   wing
    the air tremulous a   bove the tractor
would snort when it hit   gumbo

            the last   words
            i was dip   ping in but
        the lines peter   ed out
    at the end when you   had to
                lift   the pl
            ough

                            and

    turn aro
        und

~ 19 ~

        in verse and   re
               verse   veer to
            ward   words & vers

    there before us the word could   re vert again to green
        he said had grown   summoned to his days

                        2

versus, a line or row, spec. a line of writing (so
named from turning to beginning a
nother line

                        against to turn   again st
            in boustrophedron   turning
an ox writing north   of estevan
meeting the lines   head-on

                    in real   ignment re:
                        align   meant i mean
                again & again st   rain of ever
                    writing poetry for   days on
            end under the scraping est   evan sun
                        the sky on   fire
            once the lid has lif ted   & slid o
            pen the field where   it turned
                        dark   & shining
                & the thrilled gulls   in voices called
                    grey & white   let
                    ters read   eagerly
                    to one   a no

                            ther of
        fended almost the world was turning
        black under them the whiteness they brought

3

that's what   it is
to go   over
& o   ver
again to   go a
gainst the   way & so
to aver
so to a
void a vere
a swerve
a mere an   swer
i swear to god

the wild high cries
shadows on the field work
the rearranging   of pages
when they darken under the red
tractor

4

a succession of words arranged according to natural or recognized
rules of prosody and forming a complete metrical line

the love my uncle   spoke
ever a verse   in the road
i swear it is   a going
back a   turn
ing over
a turning up a   turn ip

a new   leaf
a new   line
who knew   the dew
line was the   answer
was upon   the pump
kin a pull   ing guard
a lov   ing uncle
taking   turns

```
came down    the line
down the     line he came
he was a     line man
it was an end    run
he put everything on    the line
```

5

we weren't even on the metric system
in those days it was nothing but feet

```
                      an O   penning of
                            the field
            & what if    i failed
            a sowing of    letters
            a serving    of crops
              a kind    of answer
            i swear it    was
              a goin    go
              ver &    o ver
```

```
      again it    served
   us right it    served us
right left &    centre it certain
ly did right up    to the end and down
                            to end up
                  the field shares
      & shares    a like
         a kind    of doing
         a kind of    shining
```

```
   when the words rose    in low smoky clouds
and the gulls listened    eagerly
            screamed   to one another
            moved in    a wild shindig
              & fed    avidly
   when ever some thing    would show up
            & they heard    outrageous rumours of life
```

unhitching winter

spring in harness jingles
                inside winter
bells the sky big
     chested february sun

chime of sun & snow
     itch of wool
forests of frost on windows
& wind where it eats
                        knocks cold
     out of sky
                    pops its knuckles
          swings march open

twice a year

                     each may every october i climb
                     into my father's skin & turn

the seasons over, nothing to it
  clockwise, that's spring
counter-clockwise &
                it's fall
a few twists of the pliers,
    a new season
the plumbing in   /or out

a kind of bear i guess except
my father wore these clothes
    closer than words
      when he started up
the machinery of seeds in spring
when he let may into the farm
& every fall let summer out
drained it, heat in the radiator
a leak in the year he opened
    on the green tractor pissing
    out its life when you got home late
    & it was dark in the yard
    eyes ript out of summer
    & he opened a plug in the dark
      & the cold cursing

a bit like letting a cat out for the night
into claws & whiskers whatever
suspicions of mice slept in its throat

once a year i plug the cottage in
    five months tend a yard
listen to a summer birds simmer inside
    late afternoon begins
& drags the birds out, their brightness
      & then once more

unplug it, hopeful as a farmer
at harvest & at seeding let water into place
     when trees
get tired & the heat drips out
          leaves dry as paper

sadder in fall maybe than he was
though who can tell what winter
held for him how winter held him
     bright at the window
                    when he climbed out
                    coveralls stiff at freeze-up
                    & when he climbed back in

this was when melting happened when
he climbed back into spring & wondered
where the water went when he turned around
& it was 20 below morning

cringe of morning

the trick of flies   early lives
cornsyrup clogged below my eyes
shudder   of ink

blunder of turtles   plopping off rocks
a wooden bridge   rumble of wood Allen
Yares falls   falling through
a syringe into skin
& drowns
in gravel & surprise & a truck

swinging   down air

strangely calm in the dream   or is it
heavy the memory of that
& then   swimming in the same water   after

then a pink
pearl

rubs out the charcoal
coating the eyes
swipes the black
board   clean again

a
wake &   see
the sky   unlidded
drawn
out of water   clear &
blonde
dawn
drawing upon clean
& wet   as snow

winter garden

gravestones in a winter garden: elevators
the sky having neither front
nor back bends from hand to hand

an enormous ring we are set in
easy as light or soap
a metal blue it wld take a can

opener to pry apart or punch holes in
& who is to say the boy the girl who drift
are where boats in blue would
ever be or want that blue
sea open as the beginning
& as unforgiving

the man inside glides silently
into a halo of chaff
floats up and down   gently
moves like snow in glass

line age

                    look in the mirror and
                                there he is
                    my father is
                    looking back
                            these days he is
                    more & more there

he started to show up
2 or 3 years ago
doesnt say   anything but

when i smile he smiles
when i lean over

the light stretches
my face tight for shaving
there he is   shaver in hand

it may be   a simile

            i wink   he winks back
wrinkle my forehead my eye
brows thicken his nose grows
        bigger i begin
                            to follow
in his lines
                    my age

) his eyes   look
            a lot   like mine

one morning when he hefts
the two-bushel bag   of night
before the light   i think
i will look up quickly
while hes off guard
                    & speak

im pretty sure ill find him
    talking too
              \a few words
)he was a quiet man

    but it looks like
    i am beginning to look
      a lot
          like my father
              i am beginning to
    look for my father

      look my father
    i am beginning

swept/

(a granary
            loud with wind
a wind heavy and cold in its rafters
        in grey wind
                stones of wheat
        stored in the bin
and still the strong wind
                        rolls through and
            razors
        the light

springsnow smells
                        & rats
            running
                & then the
            swallows wet
                    dripping &
            puddles of air

                the land
lasered with light
        fine green hairs
    the long loud wind

every year my dad drew lines

he may as well have drawn lots
but he never did he always drew lines
       lots & lots of them

into the land these long long lines
he would go bumping down the lane
first on the Massey & then the John Deere Dear
John he would write inbetween
      scribbled in that
stubby scrawl of huge fingers
      thick from nicotine & grease & tools
he wrote his hand over the face of the earth

           every spring he went at it writing spring
           dear spring darned glad you came back
           all winter I was wondering where you'd gone
           wrote flax wrote wheat hello
           wheat hello wrote dear barley
           wrote rapeseed once but it didn't
           write back a lot of his correspondents
           never replied some years
                he hardly heard a thing
           he'd drag those pencils across the fields
             & wait & wait
                    & wait
           he wanted to keep in touch

      in good years when he left his homework on the black
          boards wrote between the lines
            sun rhymed
                seeds green with june then
                        blond as august
this was when they carried on
some kind of correspondence
before he wrote them off altogether

most years the seeds fell silent
sometimes they'd mumble a bit
sometimes they'd hardly let out a peep
when they stopped talking
we moved into town it gets lonely
talking to yourself

                    god knows
    he yearned for a word from them
    any word wondered had his letters
    never got through was it the wrong
    address had the earth moved left
    no forwarding address every spring
    my dad wrote them in a fever
    he was in love these were love
    letters he wrote every spring had they
left him for another couldn't they do him a favour
my father grew more & more hurt they didn't answer

Worcester, Mass
Feb 29/04

                              in this day
                    of the leap
                    year i pull
          my shirt over
and i can smell my father
          who a quarter
century ago died at 68
                    born on the 7th day
                    of the 7th month
                    the 7th child
all he would have wished fallen in
to the cavity in his blood
the brevity of our blood

who dug & seeded & cleaned
his life in earth tugging
teasing & moving it
in the end falling into it
as we all will fall into

        the stories of those
whose lives were warped or dammed
                              from then until now
                              from there unto here
        where i live have lived
for 25 years women have said

they have been held in arcs
the words burnt and marked them
and others many others
those who have followed
their words and skins
where they took them

the people whose skin is so dark
it shines like chocolate
and in mathers' store i stared
   and my dad said
dennis and I knew

               and i know
   other lives wobble
looking for faces their faces
       snapt shut shut down
the smashed feet of fox and muskrat
who wander down the spoors of their hunger

i know all this and this
is true and i know my father
         fell into never
           with no word of complaint
         fell from his silence
           into silence

schemes of meridian

cactus thistle practice epistle cat tails coat tails red coats talis man
tall men some bearded some apostles white men wade through
light nearly mire in sloughs under grasshoppers that thud against
tents eat paint & wood slugs that move alongside reeds mallards
billiards honky tonk tonk tonk sun above the trestle blisters at the
correction line sublime sub liminal & you 75 years later well limbed
spun off 47 at the line that is telling tales the clock telling time
geese their watery passage scarcely to be checked hardly to be borne

troops move in traps
    in tropes lope by
surveyors scheming in meridian

the moonlight they bottle in a still by night

& huddle over

    obsidian wind outside
      its gritty blasts
    hit the smoky rooms
        sip little bits of moon
    fugitive with hope sometimes

gulp it down

July 25, 1874

*We reached Roche Percée. This singular rock is a white sandstone
of wind formation, running up like a crest from the bottom of the
Souris Valley. At its base it measures about 35 feet in height and the
base about 140 feet. Some parts are softer than others, and from the
combined influence of wind and rain, fissures and holes have been
worn through it. On different parts of the rock are cut the names of
people who have passed by and many hieroglyphics which, of course,
remain a mystery to us.*

—Henri Julien

graffitti of their movement
    with sestants & trans
      its tele
        scopes quad

rants & quills with numb
                              ers & letters
in chart & report & graph the re:
        arranging naming   real i
                                gning to things
        a scribbling of names
smoke rising from among within

McDougall NWMP
18 __

                        tattooed onto
                the hides of sandstone
            where it woos shadow
            where in may the sun is
                        a glowing concern
        & in july shrapnel
        a mortar & pestle sun

nothing like the misted hills Percy sought
& thought when spring was near at hand
                        at Roche Percée :

:

        (the pierced rock
     the wind has torn & wears as an earring
     & for centuries wore away
     the wind ringing in ears
       as over the dry grass
         the sun bent
       & wrote in small leaf & seed
       & the snow   blew in   blew out

Rawch Percy we call it
where McDougall & his troop
wrote themselves into their own Western
just south of *Bean Fate* this was
   or would in later years be

those from other grasslands
  who burrowed & pried
carbon out of the earth
badgers digging for blood
put their faith in beans too i expect

               McDougall neither well
                 done nor well
              had it seems written over
              where the deer & the buffalo lay

 but did he write off the sun & those
lines others had stained
by which they were sustained

he might well have written alongside
     never wishing to efface
        the other troops too
sensing the suns the buffalo the hands
etching etching into the softness
     not wishing to mar
or touch where their hands had drawn

ghosts we can faintly see
if at all now & then
in certain light
    late in day or filtered
shapes float up

  beneath initials of the lovelorn
those who for a moment felt a catch
in their breath wanted to say they were here
the bored the uncertain   the frightened   the stricken
the felt insignificance that wrote itself
    into the soft red

        the granite and quartz far to the northeast
          that shed inscription
        Sproxton's head a curling
        rink rumbling with rocks

                said they were   here

cenotaph
fr kenos empty + taphon tomb

i

an empty tomb
who then risen
rinsed in weak november
sun the head stone there the names
two sets of them & the men
buried there not there here
when they called

their names a skim of sno
& feet in rubber boots
air chill air thin as kerosen
school kid on remembrance y
stamping from foot to foot &
the South Saskatchewan Reg ent
loved and were loved & now

time ,old crow, flaps in our coa
& time was in the tomb
beside it ten years earlier
when there was only one list

HILL 70 ARRAS PASSCHEND LE
AMIENS CAMBRAI MONS YF
STELOI SOMME COURCECET
VIMY RIDGE HILL 80 the letters

leak into stains below &
my god the lists

ii

they must have shone there the mounties
bright as coral as blood
stones all those corporals

they must have looked like poppies &
bright tunics the yellow stripes
they stemmed the flood on
the capitals they spelt in september air
before the coal miners died inside
the long line the rifles wrote
comic book balloons bang bang
cowboys & indians all over again

wet stutter of their anonyms
their ink spilt in dust
they knelt & dug & died in
their ink spelt their deaths
in dusk they knelt & dug & died in

they were the tangled letters their names
fell into The Mercury splat they split badly
mangled & they started into history

before other uniforms & other names
    fell before not grey /red
names that never went on the stone

on other stones we read: **MURDERED
BY THE RCMP** chiselled & removed &
later yellow thanksgiving weekend
painted yellow again on the grave
stones Bienfait cemetery & went on
in minds the men who fell they tell
in dust & wind & fear & caveins
            & littered the stories we told

P. MARKUNAS N. NARGAN J. CRYSHKO
    (AGE 28)   (AGE 28)   (AGE 29)

earth swallowed them like a blotter
there is no beauty here only
somebodies story corrected in red

iii

and the cenotaph we stood
before was it '52 the perfect
symmetry this would be the miners
in '32 except i see now it was
'31 (Sept 29) Dieppe in '42 (Aug 19) no
symmetry a stone pillar & on it the dead
where i stood feet freezing in high rubber boots

May 1 / 89 writing this

their names in bronze columns
those long columns of names
i stumble on in photos

& the coroners report years later
     finally on the other corner
flanking the courthouse on the other corner

                    at the trial later many did not know
)the utter symmetry of it triangulated
                cenotaph & coal car kitty corner on 4th
they did not know what
in English they were saying

from Bienfait a new monument a coal car raised
     September 29th, 1981
it must have been a bright morning an Estevan
day dedicated to the miners
          and at the rising of the sun
          and the going down the clear
          high pain of it the way sounds hit
          when birds bang past their cries
          somebody elses breath getting
          lost in horn or bugle or coronet

& the ones who died that moment a veteran
who did not die wrote *they are
defiling British Institutions*

~ 43 ~

                              on the earth
            passing through
                              late-comers left their marks
      with penknife sentiment
                        erased the sediments of pigment
                                    & what?   fling?
      beneath their markings of territory
            their pissing on bushes
                  their trail of kleenex & condoms
            by now hardly able to find
      what for hundreds of years
      spoke to bear called on coyote
      listened to sun where it warmed the rock
      lifted their faces to the stinking sweat & blood of buffalo
      the shit & shaking earth & bellows & flies & splintered bones

            faint markings you might be able
                  to make out from over here
                        or perhaps   there
                              where you
                                          stand

eli

        all that time eli

              all that time

       you were a medicine

man it all began in est

evan 7 miles from the med

icine line a sick & blighted

      town a birth

mark a river in your temple

                 even then

         it could have been egypt

           and perhaps was

    1922 it was & later

    your pleasure when i said

    i too was born there

          / in 44

& a friend from france said "est au vent"

at least I'm not from "est au vent" cooley

       ...

   in 7 years the world buckled over on its knees

     farms were lungs collapsing

   fell onto thistles sharper than your father's razor

   everywhere houses stood with their eyes poked out

    stared out of stricken brains

      whose crevices you followed

      into the souris valley

      secrets you went in & out of

   river a bend in your head

      & **bangbangbang** they shot

          holes in the three miners

          under the hard estevan sun

          let the river out of them too

cicatrice the book says *is a scar*
left by the formation
of new connective
tissue over a healing
sore or wound.

...

& then through collapsed farms to regina its depression
streets of pharmacy
before the war & after
the unspeakable sickness you came down with
came back carrying
on your back a parcel & in your mind
a camera you could never deliver

the artist a sick man who would heal
the world's contagion coming down
with yeats & auden in a con
verted hospital visions
in slow or sudden catastrophe
krankenhaus the germans call it

let me not be crazy for poetry you wrote
a black and secret man you liked
to say you were coming
down with poetry
its unsettling inflections with which you were
badly infected
almost certain
ly inflected in strange syntax

pharm pharmacology pharmaceutical a dealing in drugs
a prescribing of poison gnosis a special knowledge a practicing of
witchcraft medicinal *pharmakon,* a drug + *poiein,* to make (see POET)
an authoritative book on the medicinal use of drugs

a dispensing then a dispen sation

...

                                    your return to estevan
                    23 & then 40 years
            later a mute in
    transigent place you in transit
        said that
                            though it listed before
        wind & dust seldom listened
        not for a minute

                you stood what? 5,7?
        gnomic watch over the wind
    & at times comically you your own comic
        ally accompanied your self

                laying down two tracks
        among weeds & dry grass
    bent over Hebrew leaning in to Cree
    learning to say what we have for
    gotten or no longer care to know

    7 miles north of the 49th meridian
            the 49 states arrayed below
        the magic line surveyors divined
    was thought by some to protect those north of it
    the world cryptic & closed with messages
                denied the word's stoney passage

                        everywhere you looked
                            a rhyming eli
                            a terrible thing

        ...

        a 7 x 7 country & you too
        beside yourself with return
        must have been next to yourself

49 your own
double mad with vexation
troubled with vision
the danger of mirrorly living

your pleasure in correspondence
& the & that sits under
the 7 on the key board
the world clicking with signs

messengers came to you
red stones in their heads & hands
& whizzed slingshots round
your head you wrestled & left

the river in your brain words swam
my grampa & i who who had been
scrolling in it
you hauled out at Possum's bridge
pulled home in a dusty trunk
not knowing we were in your head
all that time we were on your mind
that you were thinking us already
playing possum

...

& when at last the world began to hear
something at your mind started knocking
something in your head broke
it caved in knocked out
your voice in electrical storm snapt
and the world grew even more
misaligned more disfigured

the worst punishment a jew could suffer you said
who in war worked in allied intelligence
listened to clandestine whisperings
the buzz & rumble of terrifying liaisons

opened i expect & with your tongue sealed
envelopes & later reported
heard & spoke in tongues the ears' suspicions

remembering when sounds were small rocks whirled
over head into the stars flung
now slung onto
the darkness of our lives

was to have his tongue torn out to lie
in unspeaking deep as swans on the mosel
by the souris you said sorrow in Hebrew was close
to mourning close to despondence

when at last you came down with silence
your mind was a rock you could not climb over
& so you slid
inside on the canoe on the silver dollar
over the still water
its quiet shine

the rocks & the jackfish & then
you died in the world's conflagration

...

listen you said
listen
you were standing there

alone, i think

east of the wind

album

pool of electricity fallen
from the bulb the arm
brown and soft
hairs where it's broken
the paper, the light
that would have been
the colour of albumin
there & not there

open the book falling
light falling out opens
scraps of light

scraped off faces
determined as wood
& cornered there
pages of them
all the solemn faces
staring into eternity

correction line

Provisions in the rectangular survey (government survey) system
made to compensate for the curvature of the earth's surface. Every
fourth township line (at 24-mile intervals) is used as a correction
line on which the intervals between the north and south range
lines are remeasured and corrected to a full six miles.

it was at the correction line
they made their mistake
big mistake you might say

you could hear them   winding up
this would have been two or three
miles north of alison's
motors whining like giant mosquitoes
sun jumping off their windshields

they could have been on a mission
their eyes fixed on distant things
dust rising as it must have
when the israelites flew
across the desert & the camels
in hot & stinking pursuit
& the air wavered in the heat til you
weren't sure

a matter of convection surely
the sky in july an oven &
their firm conviction they would make it through
/february too

they were masters of all they surveyed &
they'd crank the mercs up tighter than the hubs of hell
round the big slough south of macleods
their hearts racing on meridians of desire
and straight ahead they'd hit the curve at over a hundred

it was then the gravel on the shoulder would grab them

                a heavy slur

                                    soft drumming &
                    /full stop
                                        that's it/
they're shit-out-of-luck in the ditch
            /period

                                & out he'd go

    my uncle walter from where he'd witnessed their wreck
            patient editor discreet confessor he'd read this stuff before
            heard their embarrassed & angry protests
            their cries of stunned incomprehension
                            & sometimes shaken
                    their sins of O! & come
            mission he feared they would never change

under the percussion cap others called sun
beside the cold granite boulder they said was moon
    inside the spinning seasons
he would drive down from his yellow
            house &   pull them
                                    out
            those that lived   out with a sigh

    on his 44 massey & his hernia
                        not a word out of him
                not a word of a lie any
    one else wld've had a conniption fit
                            but not him
    he had no misconceptions

                he'd sling   a chain
    from tractor to car shake the music
                    out of it & send it rattling
        through the parenthesis that bent in the form of a clevis
    his knees wet where in mud he knelt
            ,a comma, hooked onto
                the jangled syntax of their understanding

                            ~ 52 ~

their principle & insubordinate clauses

& out he'd   drag them   them & their concussion
                    no ifs ands or buts
            he'd bring to a sort of conclusion
                a node in their skinned-knee lives

                    this was after
        he'd found them where they had slithered
                    heavily to the side lost
        control slid off the road and sometimes rolled
            in a soft rattle   a slew of gravel
                    seized by the curve
        panic spilling their oildark words their lives
                rewritten & sometimes erased in an inky spray

            and sometimes in dark red lines at the edges
        as if someone had been making corrections
            on the windows & all over the dust-covered dashboard
                some of them still conscious

                and from my uncle
            not a word of disapproval
                not a sign of persuasion
                absolving them of their sins
                the slowness of the swift
                who though they sped
                did not prosper

                                    out he'd haul them
                        on #47 just north of estevan
                            where the gravel built up

                    funny thing is
                they never seemed to learn
                a thing about the road
            they hadn't an inkling to tell the truth
        they didn't have a clue   no conception whatsoever

                nor as for that the world either

they didn't make one single concession
clung to their skewed thinking
the world ought to be straight & fast

not a word of a lie
nothing gave them pause not even
where the spinning globe made a little side
ways hiccough
a small slither or heave   in time
a quick lurch to find itself
the turn my uncle knew
was a swerve of poetry
if not a curve he (good eye) was ready
to hit   or catch
& in his prime almost always did

never fail they would always fail
to make the turn
to make the connection
they were hell bent on getting there
where ever there was there was some thing and
hadn't a clue not one iota they didn't
give a tinker's damn about taking any other
line without a word
of a lie they plain missed the turn
misread the lay of the land

shit bad luck they would say
they'd caught a bad break
when it threw them off
\   again

& in no time back
they'd be back again   utterly unchastened
pig-headed readers   ~~deaf dead~~ bad poets
no respect for the line
where it goes or where it   breaks
none what so
ever

est au vent

its not true of course
            but in that tent where they
had the magic that's where
                        he'd go
            every summer peak
        cap & sun
                burn on his head
into a canvas bin in the prairie
            when winds would foam & sun
                        a snare
        drum would beat

    stricken he heads straight for the slide
            silver in hand
        & then is it fainter a band playing hes in
where some people no children please
            pay for a side tent he doesnt dare
        fat ladies with hair people
            stick swords or say
in another tent words eat heads off chickens

            a man turn cards
in air into other cards discard
            do quick things with coins turn
            things into other things
            houdini could not have done
better when motorcycles roar in his chains
        the way his body bent or the mirrors
                        turn bodies into waves and the cries
        girls when their bodies go into & onto the night
            something in them he doesnt understand

and when he feels as if hes had it he
        throws his voice
                    it seems so easy

standing there with sailors
hats or sleeves &

bingo

it would bounce from the outer peak
this high strange thing a squeak hidden there
or held till they let it go
a yell come down
the bottom of a long nose
the vents into & out of their heads

: one who speaks
not in wind wound
nor of wind   but
from the belly words from the belly out
—eloquent quaint billets
doux he has half a mind to

he can still hear in
side where it folds
an accordion & some times
from his mouth & out
side the queazy blink as if theyve come up out of
the orpheum in the windy light & heads

birds when they crash into glass
mirrors of their own worlds

flighty gulls
a sweet scary mystery
upon them or in them hidden
not knowing

they can throw
and sometimes hear them

death row

                                     at window   listen window
                                glass thickswollen this thick

          kids on cowpies & coalpiles
          with roundmetal lids
          looking thru them
                              dropt
          flights of bubbles bent glass
                        whistling down
                        & holding the light
          beads our fingers magnified
          sprinkling like water

   spiders   crickets   centipedes
      dry & woollen
                        sticks tick

wait you can smell in cornerdust
black in their sins their skins
shucked off within your eyes
          incinerator
                up up 7 miles into
        insect summer a kid   the sky the awesome
in summer caught the bugs   clouds go
puffed them out to curls of bacon
                a cure
          Aug 6 504,000 (of them)
             the CBC says
bombed as. i write. (just
 a baby then 1945   my sister was on her way
     3 weeks later a Little Boy   to the beauty parlour
37 years later Lake Winnipeg   when you touched her
and the radio saying the plan (no : the plane)
  Babies satisfactorily born blessed Trinity   the skin came off
blood gggusssshh gguuuusshh thru your eyes on your hands and it
& hands that type held the prisms   was black she died
  the glass prisons magnifying   in 4 days

~ 57 ~

glasses hot under hotsun under

       persons blinked
puffed in one bonesnap
    said By the neck   it was like the sun
my god my God Mathers sd   had crashed and exploded
                   their backs torn
my god his hair their   open so you could see
hair jumps white pitches white   their backbones my mother's
at breakneck speed   entrails hanging out

I am become Light
The Shatterer of Words

(you can gas them too
)   Had it coming
      I guess.

       so you bend the glass you blent in
       visible in inevitable white
       inevitable death
         magnify the whites

    they will twitch
    dance the light their tight
rope bodies on wires hum   As "demonstration"
  & smoke jump to vapour   it would be kind
              of a "show."
    The neck may
  God almighty man white
hair his white white hair
may he wilt my god lordship necrophilia
         spectral in glasses
    dark all dark burning all day   some were missing
        brightly   their eyes   my skin
skip then & dance light   was hanging like slime
    the fantastic light   like a rag
    you listen to me the light   a rag from my left arm
      a dimpled lad

lead if you lean right and splash
    your eye in lungs

                      broken when
                      when
                        like a baby

          shake it (up) now baby
     dance the spastic
          light   plastic
            spas tic
                    light

           tac
  tic

      pan
        ic
     tic
      tic

              tic

                tic

tic

there between

shot marbles
every spring it would be march
and snow on the ground
or april and the snow
in banks of coarse salt
melted against the school
the heat on
the brick & stone knew
it was time

so did the ducks that
crashed on the ice
skidded like snow planes

we would blow on our hands
kneel on the wet spots
breathe & rub the marbles
snap of thumb squirt of light &
the lovely click of glass on glass

at home we would take them
bags full & feel them
their smoothness & squeak when we squeezed
and in tobacco tins the loud crashings
& the water swished
down culverts put corduroy in the water
and the sloughs smelt wet
the reeds dull and flat

held them
the ones of one colour
pale blue and amber faint green
up to the light up to the window
saw in them suns and stars
bright things in their galaxy
a clarity that later clouded
we later learned
to call love

in estevan

the sun never misses
a step never stops
running that it is all you need
to know that and that
it rams into day
slams into earth

ticks by   a windmill by day
it clicks night away in a movie reel
all you need do is
reach up &
switch it /on
but you must be

careful always to step back stand clear
there can be no catching
the meter racing
the speed of light

night a stain spilled & spreading
saturn that lumpy old turnip
is a top turning
our dreams on rheostat
brings them up
rocks in spring
every evening down
it reams day out
our dreams all night long
bump into one another
rafts cut loose in a harbour

nudge through all the doors & windows
in estevan

the clocks we lock & choke in

                              in side the bones
                              the lonely bones
                              long as time stick
                              & unstick wheels
                              go with & out crank
shafts shift shin & skin
the pain locked in its side
look inside see pins tumble sounds knock
        stumble inside the stomach want out

time is stranded in strangled voices
in streaks & it stains the pine box
the orange cat hisses & steps by

pockplock bones talk
loud horses they walk over
the floor its sweat shines
they boom & bang doors shut grates
stoves rattle inside their dark skin
    wrapt round tobacco breath
the dark stairribs click & hold

        grampa coughs the springs
        noise through the oil
        darkness slings time slowly past
        puts rhymes in brass &
        grampas iamb grampas bad
        back gramps back with his cuffs

his cough barely swerves wears its muscle inside out
in knitwool sweaters grampas finger bones feel
the way elm trees feel when they stand
their faces splotchy in the middle of day

spills shadows stiff ones & moving
hang onto the wall at night once the air
strains with listening bangs wide
awake at the door i watch & read them

the bones have got out their whiteness
cast it on the wall the floor they bunch
            in the hallways *thickthick*
        drive nails all night long
                into our sides

there she was

there she was pen in hand hinted opined actually she had other
things to do way better things to spend her time on than waiting
at the correction line where dust spun the sky & turned in a
small tornado halo if you prefer sunstained cars in slow motion
rolled already bleaching among the buffalo bones & saskatoons
that stained her hands she surveying all theyd done she in her
carefully kept portfolio insisted on all the right corrections &
bloody well had the red ink to show for it she was ready for
accident or negligence whichever was worse or first or at hand
to sustain her & what was more she ran a tight ship surely
landbound now landblown theyd taken one trip too many had
gone too far & though they were au courant when they let her
rip for just a minute threw her off threw her a curve those ruddy
country boys were unspeakably crude & had no sense of form a
lot they cared & so she knew when the currents bore them she
would have to be firm with them straight from the farm what else
could she do it was for

their own good she would make them toe the line it was time
someone woke up those hicks and set them straight and so it fell
to her lot & she had so arraigned them she was the one had lain
down the law remained true to the one true standard meridian
in Greenwich this was and she was ready & able to put them in
their place she had been pretty temperate actually she had been
downright permissive if truth be told latitudinarian one might
say nay saying none of them up until now that is before they got
carried away on their new expeditions expectations running amok
& lost in contradictions in this dark world & wide set off on wild

indefensible paths insensible trips to paris where they stumbled
on aigu grew clumsy with ague nearly fell over circumflex & fell
into loutish outings to frankfurt outlandish lyrics très outre that
ran afoul of the umlaut for crying out loud they were courting

trouble trouble was they didnt know their place the prairie yokels seemed to have forgotten they were snorting through german beer and snuffling down french brandy till they were no more than hiccoughing in their crude lies their pretentious lines they assumed were into current things the swim of things when they whitebellyflopped into europe they thought when they were fooling around when she was in to phases of the moon phrases that were in time with eternity in tune with

proper measures in turn in truth ever returning in sooth surely had gone wrong as she was sure-footed sooth-sayer & she had gathered about her great circles drawn about her in a mantle the celestial meridian itself latterly they had taken a lot of latitude she would have to lay out the transit story once & for all lay it on the line show them precisely how & where the tides went in & out at her bidding & the trees when she spoke

or raised her hand budding too & why the lat and longed itudes met she would show them what was what & what was more what they failed to appreciate in their provincialism in not knowing the one true vertical its meridian of veracity she had with conviction drawn knowing convection too was on her side that she would ride the currents firm as a battleship in prow adorning twice as steady over the hot

ripples of fields & fads destined to fade like sunken lorries where she dropped charges (they were deep & final) for she was not going to be sorry she would avoid the transitory in no way uncertain she would keep in touch with forever the straight & hoary that which was the long & the short of it & by them she had them firmly she would have to teach them a thing or two straighten them up turn them from their crooked & wayward habits their bad form though she had taken a small hit below the water line that was why she was not

shy she's never shied & never would shed a tear for any of them & why she summoned them once and for all rubbing their eyes on one foot then on the other stood some of them having to leave the room & because there was a lot on the line dirty linen

certainly some one or ones had exceeded their alloted earthly
spheres upon the world that turned &

whirled like a turnip & there decamped on her majety's domains
squatted & there was a lot to get straight not much to go on or
to go around where she had them squirming had them just where
she wanted them they who could not wait to tie one on she had
left dangling there from there to here to the correction line she
had caught them red-handed & dead-wrong in her deictics though
they sang in their chains like the crows

to the north

by the river in the valley
the graves have lost their markings
natives and miners and unmounted police lie
among frecklings hide in shade beneath saskatoons
and the elms rise like children's arms along the souris
not knowing they soon will be eaten

the trees to the north are dense
the narrow rings they laid down each year
stunted from all that heat in the sky
squeezed so hard they are
making their way
slowly to coal

the trees writhe and feed on
people in the painting you can see
in yellow and blue twisting you
can hear the colours
the shrill waves in air
pebbles & small flowers on blue
gamma you can see all
the way to weyburn and back
and inbetween birds notch the air
& the air snaps
apart their wings

they're about to turn into the entrance
about to turn
on the no vacancy sign
the hotel almost filled with tenants
the open-air rooms provided with stone
pillows & sheets pulled up over their heads
under which their thoughts forever lie

light & dark piled there
the tunnels of their throats closed
trying to block out the noise of our visits
    sound of us in gravel
trying hard to keep their dreams from rising

who could reproach if they suspected
    we might step on them

who be surprised if they turn
    baffled faces filled with fear
we will tear the membranes from their ears
        who can blame them
        if they want to close their eyes

    feel only the sky's short blowings
        feel moons wobble through like blood clots
    the wind up to our ears in our hair
    knotted in small embraces
           bright ghosts of the living
           the living and the dead

when school is out

high into night into candle
sticks furred with blue

far as anyone can see
an electric eel is unfurling
        the ferris wheel
    tipped on its axis reels
        our dreams a giant
            watch glows & rolls in reverse

                spools & spokes roar past
rhyme & bear
    through doors of dark
                    & light blizzards

    below the kids
        wade in yellow
    & red when they release
            the brakes & horses
        wild eyed whorl
the whole world a well of light

        the pin wheels the sun
    flowers spin the swollen night

& late at night the drive
            a dark wall

    car a finger of light
the left angle turn
            the gravel road

                up & over
                    the hill
                    the slough
                turn up the lane
                        arrive to

                linger of summer
                        the moon
                    lewd as a ladys bum
        in the yard the dark
                            dogs rub
        & the kerosene lamp serene
                    a cow   at milking
            the horses in the night pasture breathing

                                in bed
                    the rain-
        on-the-roof voices   my mother
                & my father   talking
                    farther & farther into the night

voice:

it is spring

the ground still wet

or after, later

it is hard to know

he is lying   in the pasture
part way down   the slope to the ravine
just outside estevan
just below the breeze
a catchpool for sun
he turns his face to

cups his hands &
in greeting or in question
hollers
up the rise

haa^{ay}yy

in a second
his voice

comes back

slower & deeper

hhhaaaayyyh

surprised, pleased

now he's got wind of it

he calls
again & again

*where arrrre you
are you therrrre*

the sound
bounces back

aarrrreee yyoOOOouuUuu

hhell ooooo   all looohh

claps off the barn
      its stone-grey walls
carried on wind

                  50 years later
                              he sends
            out words &

      they   barely come back
                        no answer   no other

      words   only a   small voice
            small & dampened
                        talking to itself

in tongues

sky is a tin rink
wind skated on

blink of childhood
days open
trains of memory
Montreal to Toronto
Mar 24 Via

Rail wet mitts
their cake of winter
my gramma cooley hangs
the coalstove winter drips
through camphor drips
and light bunches at the windows

on the back
step you   stoop
where sun hits
its shins   & shines
over the 25
gallon drum
its white flesh

& lick

stick tongue
-tied to metal
)dianeknelt tongue
to rail   rail to tongue
Sioux Lookout

leave white tongues behind
red tongues
in the mouth
afraid to tell
unable to speak

the heft of rocks

And so life is reckoned as nothing. Habitualization devours works,
clothes, furniture, one's wife, and the fear of war. If the whole
complex lives of many people go on unconsciously, then such lives
are as if they had never been. And art exists that one may recover
the sensation of life; it exists to make one feel things, to make the
stone stony . . .

— Victor Shklovsky

the heft of rocks the skin's abrasions
where the stones came from where they had been
where they'd slept those thousands years

his dad from his sunburned arms & neck saying
they were ploughing the pasture
were going to sow part of it
down the slope to the ravine
and that was when they hit it

    the rock all the rocks
   the tractor's shock where
the shears skinned the earth
its shining black body suddenly leapt
        their own wonder
     when they heard

    grate of steel on granite
beneath the surface where they poked
the sharp smell saw the stones
       lift like bladders
slipt from slaughtered pigs &
            fall back

    couldn't see couldn't stop
       in haste & sweat
his dad and another man he can't remember
    he may have been a LaRoque

or Pelletier

the earth softened & the air told them
it was spring it was time to sow
time to move on keep moving

told him the hills above the ravine
had once been full of graves
                    people had dug
and he had thrilled at the thought
          that there would be
arrow heads and spear tips & shocked
          anyone would dig a grave
                    a person's bones & things right there
                              for everyone to see

      small boy on top of the world
above the ravine south of the farm
the big hill in jeans & tee-shirts
we rode up wheels flashing
to town extended in a spine
long bone two ribs actually
west to east east to west
on the other side the south slope
under the grasses their wiry dust
          in pale purple & yellow
crocuses wedged & in small haloes glowed

          and at the top two lines of white
stones mottled & parallel and following
      the ridge the stiff wind
                    his face sun burning
      the wind blew through
                    hill on a high sky
                              the earth breathing
          under foot & winter
                    slid from snow so bright
      his sisters & he had to squint

felt the toboggan snag on the wolf
    willow down the side

& in Orlovsky's pasture on the other side
one summer found a bone arrowhead
    carried & later lost

but this time (it must have been may
   season of permission
         and demand
spring busy with his father & the man
       they had stood &
listened for a minute & gone
    on intended to
   come back to what
       had spoken wished
they had marked the spot
and soon let the ground go back
           lost the place
           lost their place

the sound that evaded them
slipt away as at night it did
when they we blew out the lamp
   and the light was gone

    there under the grass
             their lives circled
     in smoke & talk
    hundreds and hundreds of them
   dreaming inside hoops of skin & rocks & pictures
    rounded from where they had fallen
      from a far world its cliffs of ice
  & enormous sweeps of snow a few people
  the world turning on its axis
       water turning warmer

    the weight of those who stopped here
   just over there they are eating & dancing

& over smoking fires tanning
hundreds of years in wind and sun
thousands passing through they too
with the buffalo their rivers of flesh
drifting with the seasons from wooded clefts
in what we called the souris valley
& what they named the family did not know

   they too summoned by sun
by lives that turned in moon tuned to the hard bright stars
  revolved in grass & geese & muskrat
     squeezed through the ravine
in open fires & snow & tipis with strange things
   on them & horses that shivered
  in winter & fly time stamping
moms with pots and little kids snitching eggs
    and men with bows & the wind
  blowing as always here it did
from the west & in april cold & hard
filling the bottom of the world with water & ducks
     talked in the dusk

  would never have known they were here
and though later they would in another way know
they never would have known he wouldn't know
   at the time where they'd gone or when

at the time we could look out the kitchen window and see
  somewhere just past the barb wire
   they were that near that close

circus

ferris wheels carousels the zipper
the soft fabric of night unzips
the scrambler roller coaster round-up

thousands of children dazed turn
into something once a year
heat come out of the earth
water & air on their skin

the caramel trance they dance
the cotton candy tied to
feast beneath and eating enter

lights that buzz & fuzz
    let out dizziness

children solemnly swim the golden rings
        their lives spin
thin lines they, swimming, swallow
follow their murmurs away from home

and underneath a strange voice
        under water crying
they are to enter and to know
the dark iris behind the lights
        waits for them
and everything in growing circles moves

children of light

down & up   you go
                                      a gust of light
                            over floors in your mind
            august bridling the horses of gold
                                      & earth turns
                  wrings silver from the moon

                  *

                        children chilled
            in barrels of night
                        their fingers dip
                                    the eggshell light

                  *

            moon is
                        whirling round
            & round our heads
            a child tows
                        earth twirls & twists

                  it round & round
            & wont let go

                  earth turns
            dark & holds on to the moon
            dark bloodstone or
                  lump of blood

                  *

            children lean out
                              from dark caves
            crack open   leak grackles

beaks of men   beside them
circle & click
click & sickle something
shiny   as clocks
in their hands

the machine in the garden

sun drops off
flies on its hot dog face   lost halo
behind the lane the bottom of lane
the ditch we swam

: a squeaky sound
blurs in the patch moving
mr le blanc has scraped to life
when he isnt selling
lotions & unguents someones in the corn lynn
or is it sharon in august in sudden
seeing shoves the idea (it isnt
hard) into our heads

:

:

someone
in the garden

?should we sic the dog

crescent
because of the sickle
moon on her forehead & she the milk
cow has knelt   thru the fence shook
free &

jumped
the first glimmer of night
followed her black & white face eyes wild
poke tilted to the north

star she has climbed the world
under an aluminum moon followed
the moon in her head

a float on the pail into which light foams
some times a thick yellow mostly a watery white
she & the stars faster than jacob
have leapt under or over

the moon she's plunged to chlorophyll
squeaks when she swings
her head side to side she's run
a ramp of darkness & cracked the moon
yanks it open once she's lurched
the barb wire its heaviness
coming down & shoving
ka-**tthunk** all the way through

over her ears in corn rips the ears
slathers the night & rolls
infrared eyes
archangel burning brightly
horns & all
pilfers & shrugs
corpuscles from the electric fence roll
her shoulders
into the deepening purple & her breath
wheezes the night air

palimpsest

a maple table it will do it is ample gramma cooley's brown
skin scarred from operations time has performed a clean
        shadow it could be
a coronet from the coffee cup in small curves
leaves light & dark light & dark blur beside
interruptions you blend in

the small eruptions memory is my gramma bent at the table
sampler in hand sewing the skin a black cormorant & your empty
cup the sliver when you went where shadows shed and bleed

                  a basket of oranges & lemons
                    small sour suns that sting
                      the tongue their nipples
                        & bumpy skin

fallen out of time or into a hole a dim light so many went into &
did not come back or in flickers across chairs do come back & on
the table July 1 the broken corpse of a mosquito that squeezed in
the early evening through air thick as heat from a running dog
the threads hum to their small voltage a spidered calligraphy still
wet at the perforations in day a dark brown the lighter teapot
skin the table's burns and scratches the pores life takes its breath
through & death a cup we fill & drink the oil gives the window
light it sits on sits in time & time again lets time out in filaments
of ink their hot sting

the stone garden

sun that comes up like thunder
immensity of sky density of grave
    birds in the sky
        stain it with their quick lives
     when they turn
          the winds snap
  their wings apart

        the trees arthritic & stricken
        wood so hard
        they could be anthracite

   all winter long
  they hardly   breathe
    try to drink
  through narrow rings
   they sleep inside
a small hill north of estevan
    the summer turns
   gravel heavy as those
  it has shovelled in

              sun shoves
         them down
  into hardness
turns them into darkness
     earth straining
  the flesh we pass through

       the paper hearts
    the world like water passes through

~ 84 ~

a small boy

he is five maybe, perhaps only four
    he is dressed in darkness
brown rayon pants   belt & shirt to match

he is squinting into sun
light falls off his face onto paper
he will lean over 50 years later
rubbing his eyes, writing bits of darkness
                or erasing

but now he is mad & wishes
he was wearing jeans and tee shirt
    he does not want
        to be in the picture
        his eyes hurt

    it is the end of a hot day
the sky in front of him
        wide as helium
      except behind
the pumphouse almost frighteningly small

in the picture he is facing west
          into the sun
          into the camera
    day a delirium

          on the end of shadows
          she is holding
shadows fall out of her hands as only
    in the prairie they could

her own long shade he would stand in
where she kneels on the other side of then
  wants to take him
        into the camera
    his darkness blocking the light
she wants to take away in her pocket

he likes the shadows, they are steep & strong
longer than the time she is sliding down
though neither he nor she knows
this nor why she wants
the picture, feeling time
pressing sun at her back

he is in a sulk does not care she wishes
perhaps his hair is newly cut, it might have been
he hates the bits of hair on his neck
hates to stop & look into the sun

he knows there is a garden to her left
                    outside the picture
                    behind the picture
there would have been a garden

crowded with corn so tall he felt small & lost
there would have been all she hoped
        the day she took the pictures
behind her behind the days s/he dreamt
            this day would ever enter

behind her at the end of the lane
he will hear a voice a few years later
a clear voice out of the west sky, strong and clear,
this will be at the end of a summer day too

the large sun that hangs in the west
            every day forever
every day a door closing
in shadow he will hear
        what it says he will
    ask   did she hear too
though when he is older he will not remember
                what it said
though she will say no, his mother,
did not hear when he asks her then

he will remember where she stood
in front of the sun, see the small spot
where her body begins
            to boil over
      a geranium that overflows its pot

he will remember there were long shadows
            distinct faces, as near
      & distant as memory   / as slanted

she wants to coax a mother's picture of him

                  there is sun in his eyes
      where she stands in front of the sun
            she has disappeared into over
            -exposed to time & the picture
                  they never took of her

                  before she went away
                  walked into the picture
      before they fell out of her hands

                  & they were dissolving
                        turning to light
                  losing their shadow

wrestled with you

on the edge of the garden
corn reached over my head
surprised how easily you won &
the other time same place small kid
you pulled me out of spring
    where id sunk
down to the top of my rubber boots
where turnips heaved up summer &
rolled round gerunds out of the ground
        & cucumbers
hid themselves under cumberbands
watched from where they bristled
    in hiding the ginger
sun when it passed them by

    ruth herself stood
under wiping her forehead
corn in which she stood
sick for her lost children

dana ,leaving

someone has spoken
there is no way of knowing
who or why or what this is
but it has been

said & it spreads in spokes
along which you must move
must answer though
you would rather not

this is a place in which you are
written you feel you have
not fully authorized

Chicago it says & it says
this is where you are

going though your face says no
& your eyes
going going
do not wish it   wish
we would have spoken
another word along which
balance against falling
you could have
climbed back into

the first story the second storey
into which you strayed in which you stayed
& there would be room
whose walls said night
& day the words mothers & fathers speak
wishing to hold forever in you

where when you leave their ears will hurt
from the silence you have left behind
full of light & shadow moving
the weight of nothing on them

Megan

*

,waiting

our lives thin & precarious as light
when bulbs puncture they end
time rattles inside & wears through
explode when dropped or run
over or wear down after awhile
filaments flimsy as nerves

you on the end of our lives
something is in & they will enter
the thin membrane of your breath
your life that lifts from our throats
wanting you to float there forever
moving as moons should move
   bright & perennial as the night which turns
               into a second fullness
   stuck on the sky's high ceiling

          blue moon the man on radio says
     this is once
           in a blue moon

the warm & uneven way we stand
the uncertain waiting our breath takes
seeing you thrown onto the world's four winds
             far & fast as weather
         the seasons blowing through

no way to pull you out or hold you
here at the end of the string
luminous sky in our hands

    windy weather in all of us
    not knowing which way the winds are blowing
      or when they will end

*

night before:

three when you wakened screaming
the wolves are eating my stomach
only you couldn't say the "l" quite
said wo'ves are eating my stomach
you in my arms knowing they held you
against everything forever

lie now inside your fear
something again is eating your stomach
& you wonder though do not say is it
what ate your grandmother away
fear has thrown its switches &
a small bomb has gone off inside
& Fenrir i know is eating the moon
is eating you yellow as the jaundice
you were born into one Christmas

tomorrow they will go inside
our fear the cold in the room your small body
my father's hands i touch you with
what i know you feel at our skin
would lift this from you now
let you into sleep where you hear
my body running over
we both know there is nothing i can do
cannot scare off the wolves this night
which always before you have turned
to anger now you lie quiet
at the ends of my frightened love allow my hands
move into sleep under my face

*

dream of you as freckles:

shallow plate of your breath
shadow sparrows drink at, startled

i am thin as tin
the smallest word
could puncture
everything dust so
dry i could fall
almost with the pain
& still feel i am
so transparent
you could see
right through
the wind
on the other
side

*

at night   :

the sleep you have
bandaged yourself in
fish in the dark
waters

coming back into
your flesh
rising in
day

*

were you cold

you looked cold
you say

last night

*

, morning of

     your mother climbs the dawn
the bright wires in the streets
the last days of august swing open
more large & open than ever this summer
in the morning to braid your hair
against all unravelling to tie up ends

in whose body month after month moons drifted
till one caught & there was you

            sounds of morning rise
            our shadows on the wall
            sun across your bed
            you hold yourself in
                your body
                        blooms brightly
          with pain

though this is the seventh hour of the seventh floor
there is no one to climb your long hair to rescue
nothing to keep out the snow
not the wooden christmas decoration
our want of you hangs by the mirror in
no not your robe blue as may nor your nose
where you thought you were broken
not even your hair to protect you

     the emptiness
         of your sandals
   when you go

*

Megan, in

, the morning we go down into
everything fragile , the air
its yellow feel
always i loved this time of year
the gentle
clarity of light
brittle this time
as ice the water's drained under

in the streets people move oblivious to time almost
everything so slow
so fast
a dream you cannot want

you alone in a room full of strangers
who touch your loveliness with a strange love
a man's skilled & clumsy hands
write scars over your unknowing
puts holes in you wanting you whole

in this world they take everything away
when the winds blow moons through our hearts
our hands feel the weight of your skin not there

*

came to braid the morning
as they did the queen's
, her hair
preparing for death

*

you lie there

eyes beneath
all that darkness
its weight on your eyes